I0896592

ANIMALS OF THE FOREST

Great Gray Owls

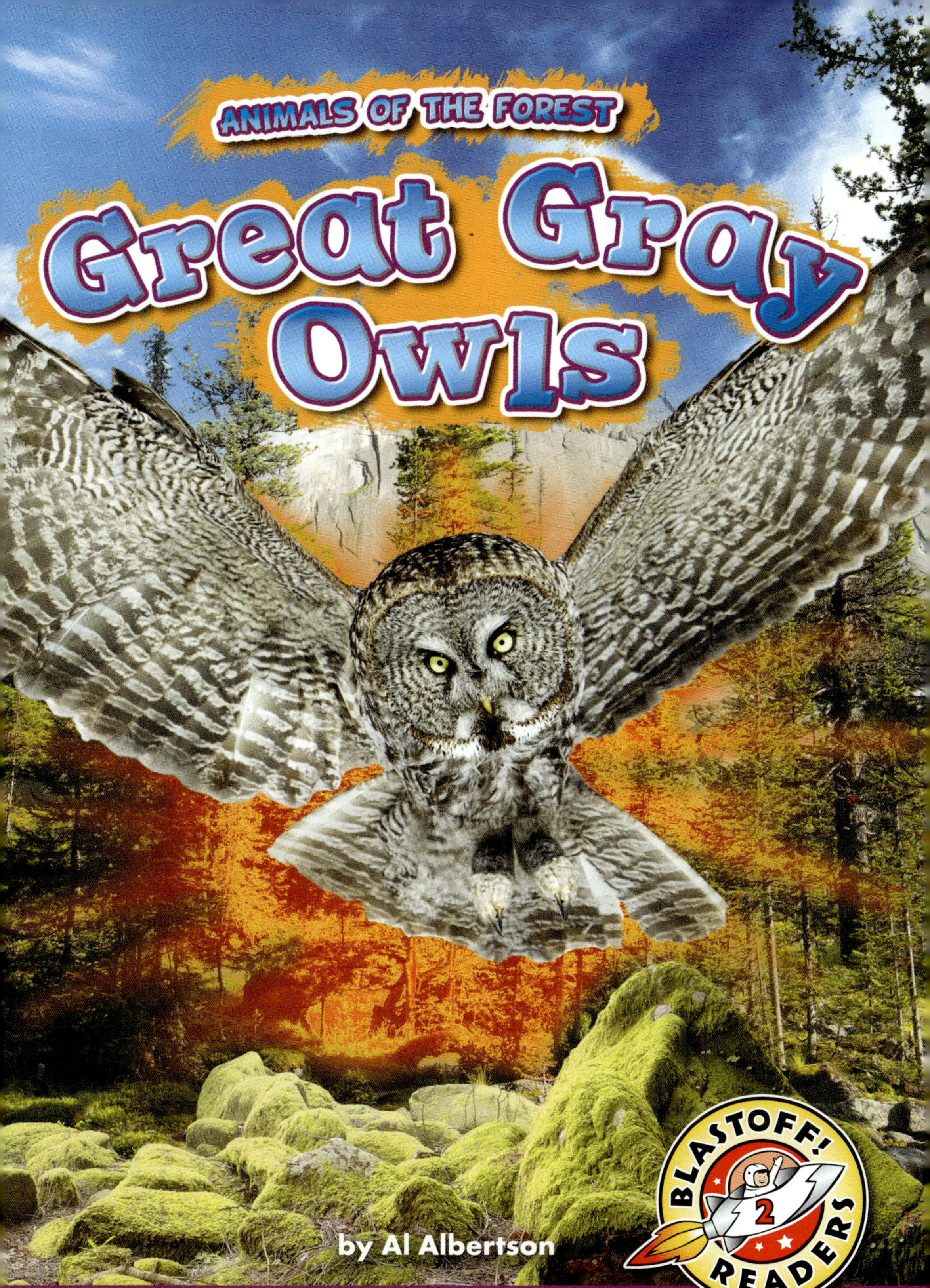

by Al Albertson

BELLWETHER MEDIA • MINNEAPOLIS, MN

Note to Librarians, Teachers, and Parents:

Blastoff! Readers are carefully developed by literacy experts and combine standards-based content with developmentally appropriate text.

Level 1 provides the most support through repetition of high-frequency words, light text, predictable sentence patterns, and strong visual support.

Level 2 offers early readers a bit more challenge through varied simple sentences, increased text load, and less repetition of high-frequency words.

Level 3 advances early-fluent readers toward fluency through increased text and concept load, less reliance on visuals, longer sentences, and more literary language.

Level 4 builds reading stamina by providing more text per page, increased use of punctuation, greater variation in sentence patterns, and increasingly challenging vocabulary.

Level 5 encourages children to move from "learning to read" to "reading to learn" by providing even more text, varied writing styles, and less familiar topics.

Whichever book is right for your reader, Blastoff! Readers are the perfect books to build confidence and encourage a love of reading that will last a lifetime!

This edition first published in 2020 by Bellwether Media, Inc.

Library of Congress Cataloging-in-Publication Data

Names: Albertson, Al, author.
Title: Great Gray Owls / by Al Albertson.
Description: Minneapolis, MN : Bellwether Media, Inc., 2020. | Series: Blastoff! readers: animals of the forest | Includes bibliographical references and index. | Audience: Ages 5-8 | Audience: Grades K-1 | Summary: "Relevant images match informative text in this introduction to great gray owls. Intended for students in kindergarten through third grade"-- Provided by publisher.
Identifiers: LCCN 2019024605 (print) | LCCN 2019024606 (ebook) | ISBN 9781644871270 (library binding) | ISBN 9781618918031 (ebook)
Subjects: LCSH: Great gray owl--Juvenile literature.
Classification: LCC QL696.S83 A43 2020 (print) | LCC QL696.S83 (ebook) | DDC 598.9/7--dc23
LC record available at https://lccn.loc.gov/2019024605
LC ebook record available at https://lccn.loc.gov/2019024606

Editor: Betsy Rathburn Designer: Josh Brink

Printed in the United States of America, North Mankato, MN.

Table of Contents

Life in the Forest

Great gray owls are large birds. They fly through northern forests.

The owls have **adapted** well to this large **biome**.

Great Gray Owl Range

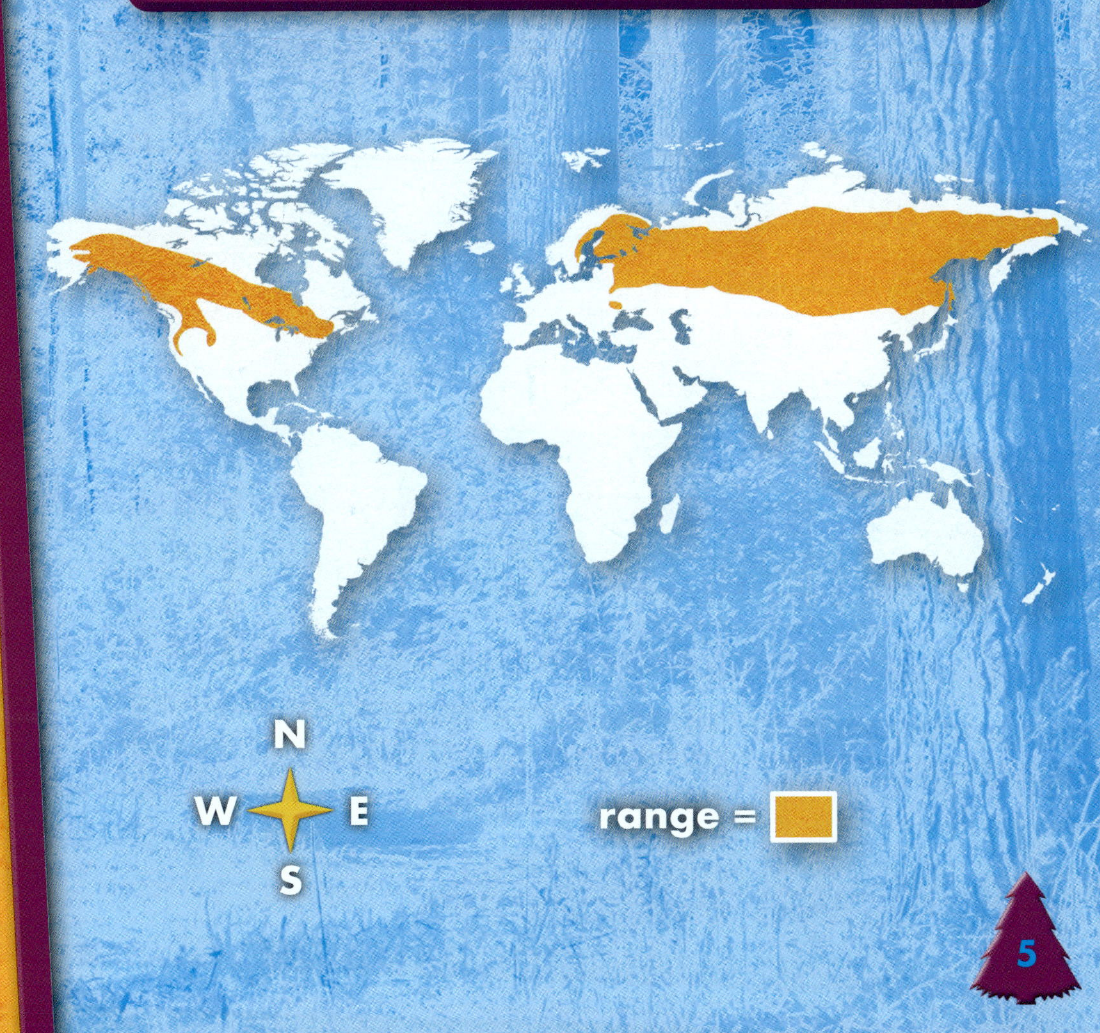

The forest is full of noise. **Facial discs** help the owls gather sounds.

Asymmetrical ears help find the direction of the sound.

These owls can turn their heads in almost a complete circle!

They spin their heads towards quiet sounds. They can even hear mice under snow!

Northern forests have cold winters. Puffy **plumage** keeps great gray owls warm.

Special Adaptations

Their feathers are white, gray, and brown. These colors help the owls hide in tall trees.

Quick and Quiet

Huge eyes help the owls see in dark forests. Wide, **fringed** wings help them fly quietly.

They slip between trees without a sound!

Great gray owls are quiet. But they still **communicate**.

They hoot to claim **territory**. Their low hoots can be heard 0.5 miles (0.8 kilometers) away!

Great Gray Owl Stats

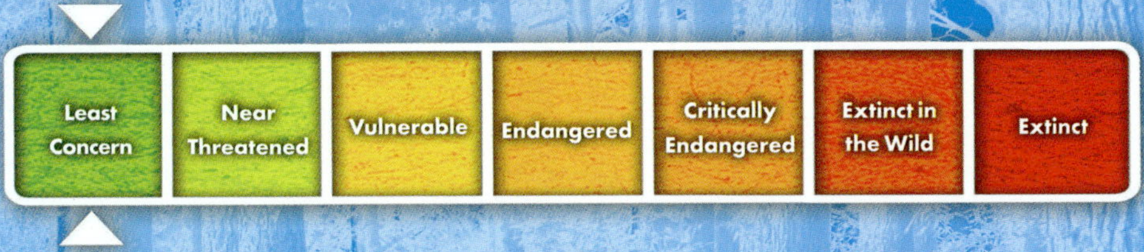

conservation status: least concern

life span: up to 13 years

Some **predators** come too close. Great gray owls scare them away.

They spread their feathers and show off their sharp beaks.

Beaks and Talons

Great gray owls hunt around sunrise and sunset. They listen and watch for **prey**.

When **rodents** come near, the owls dive feet first to catch them!

Great Gray Owl Diet

deer mice

voles

pocket gophers

Their strong **talons** scoop up food. They swallow small prey whole!

They use **curved** beaks to tear into larger prey. Great gray owls are strong forest hunters!

talons

Glossary

adapted—changed over a long period of time

asymmetrical—uneven

biome—a large area with certain plants, animals, and weather

communicate—to share thoughts and feelings using sounds, faces, and actions

curved—curled or rounded

facial discs—the parts of owls' faces that are raised on the edges and curve inward

fringed—having edges made up of thin, loose feathers

plumage—the feathers of a bird

predators—animals that hunt other animals for food

prey—animals that are hunted by other animals for food

rodents—small animals that gnaw on their food; mice, rats, and squirrels are all rodents.

talons—claws

territory—the land area where an animal lives

To Learn More

AT THE LIBRARY

Bodden, Valerie. *Owls.* Mankato, Minn.: Creative Education, 2013.

Jaycox, Jaclyn. *Snowy Owls Are Awesome.* North Mankato, Minn.: Pebble, 2020.

Sommer, Nathan. *Owls.* Minneapolis, Minn.: Bellwether Media, 2019.

ON THE WEB

FACTSURFER

Factsurfer.com gives you a safe, fun way to find more information.

1. Go to www.factsurfer.com.
2. Enter "great gray owls" into the search box and click 🔍.
3. Select your book cover to see a list of related web sites.

Index

The images in this book are reproduced through the courtesy of: Michelle Lalancette, front cover (great gray owl), p. 21; Zacarias Pereira da Mata, front cover (rocks); vladimir salman, front cover (background); Aleksey Stemmer, pp. 2-3; Artiste2d3d, p. 3; rokopix, p. 4; Roland Eriksson, p. 6; Alan Tunnicliffe, p. 7; georgesanker.com/ Alamy, p. 8; Nature Picture Library/ Alamy, p. 9; Glass and Nature, pp. 10, 11, 17; Andrea Izzotti, p. 11 (inset); Harry Collins/ Alamy, p. 12; Dagmara Ksandrova, p. 13; Chris Humphries, p. 14; Ondrej Chvatal, p. 15; Stanislav Duben, p. 16; RobinEriksson, p. 18; Danita Delmont, p. 19 (left); Rudmer Zwerver, p. 19 (right); La Renaissance Girl, p. 19 (bottom); Buiten-Beeld/ Alamy, p. 20; Agnieszka Bacal, p. 23.